One God
One Message
One Day

40 Days of Uniting with God

NIKKI GEORGE

jt publishing house

JT Publishing House

One God, One Message, One Day: 40 Days of Uniting with God
Copyright © 2023 by Nikki George

Requests to the author for permission should be addressed to:
JT Publishing House, writing@jtpublishinghouse.com

Names: George, Nikki.
Title: One / Nikki George.
Description: Spartanburg: JT Publishing House, 2023. | Summary: "One God, One Message, One Day pushes us to pursue the heart of God--the God who desires to have oneness with us. As you read, reflect upon your individual life stories and trace the hand of God in your life, guiding you to become one with the Father. "-- Provided by publisher.
Identifiers: LCCN 2023937966 (print) | ISBN 978-1-954624-17-7 (paperback) | ISBN 978-1-954624-18-4 (ebook)
Subjects: BISAC: Religious / Christian / Devotional & Prayer
LC record available at https://lccn.loc.gov/2023937966

Disclaimer: Any internet addresses (websites, blogs, etc.) and telephone numbers in this book are offered as a resource. They are not intended in any way to be or imply an endorsement by JT Publishing House or the author, nor does JT Publishing House vouch for the content of these sites and numbers for the life of this book.

Published by JT Publishing, Spartanburg, South Carolina
www.jtpublishinghouse.com

Printed in the United States of America
10 9 8 7 6 5 4 3 2 1

Table of Contents

Getting Started

There was a sound of the mighty, rushing wind one morning as I sat in quiet awe. Taking in the beauty of the overlook at Wiseman's View was breathtaking. As the wind blew, it carried a ponderosa pine that lay gently and unexpectedly on my shoulder. I observed the pine's rich, pencil wood color, dressed as one bundle with three branches stemming from it.

This moment was so symbolic for me because I had been thinking about the intangible concept of oneness. The three-in-one little bundle immediately brought the Trinity of God to mind, a message the Divine highlighted in subsequent dreams and visions. The message of oneness and unity kept driving me back to the Bible and how one life can be affected by one message that all leads up to one day.

I witnessed nature proclaim God's existence that day in the North Carolina mountains. I began to wonder how we display oneness with the Father.

Many have thrown up their hands and don't believe we can be united. I almost did the same thing. As I looked around the world, the division in churches that profess Jesus, and the divorce rates of the people who both claim Jesus, are startling. I almost lost hope until I remembered that Jesus prayed that we would become one.

Jesus said the Father always hears Him. Jesus already accomplished something great in the fact that He died for our sins in order to reconcile us back to the Father. Many know that God loves us; now it's time to return love to God by sacrificing and crucifying our divisions and becoming one with Him and each other.

There is high expectation that as we take this journey together, we will be closer to the Father. I'm praying this assignment will create an undeniable hunger to know the God of the Bible, who asserts to be the one true God, in a more intimate way, to help us outshine the things that oppose our oneness with Him.

As we look to God for direction and seek Him for understanding our destiny, He will show us where we fit in, identify our place, give us the message to share, and give us the actions to take to become one with Him and with each other.

We were created in God's image and after His likeness. Jesus' mission was and is to bring us back into reconciliation with the Father. In His final prayer, He prayed that we all would become one.

As you read, I have shared my story of becoming one with God. I encourage you to reflect on our individual life stories and become aware of and yield to the drawing we have been experiencing from God throughout our lives.

As we delve into the threads and fibers of what one life, one message, and one day allude to, we will draw closer to God as we seek Him and gain ways to personally interact with concepts and scriptures that point us towards oneness. Engage with the questions in the "Becoming One" section at the end of each devotional.

Together, let's consider and see the hand of God on and in our lives. There is an

awakening to the pull of destiny and purpose
gleaned by looking through life and seeing
the patterns, the repeated message spoken
through life's situations, circumstances, and
God's word.

We are becoming one.

One God

One God

We see miracles, signs, and wonders when we honor God's oneness. 1 Corinthians 8:6 reads, "Yet for us, there is one God, the Father, from whom are all things and for whom we exist, and one Lord, Jesus Christ, through whom are all things and through whom we exist."

God has so many names that we can spend in depth time just thanking and praising Him over His different names and attributes. He is the great I AM, Healer, Restorer, Comforter, Friend, Guide, Teacher, Way-maker, Confidant, Redeemer, Sustainer, Fixer-upper, Protector, Lifter of our head, Strength, Savoir, and the list continues.

<u>Our Prayer</u>
Our Father,

who art in heaven,
hallowed be thy name;
thy kingdom come;
thy will be done
on earth as it is in heaven.
Give us this day our daily bread;
and forgive us our trespasses
as we forgive those who trespass against us;
and lead us not into temptation,
but deliver us from evil.
For thine is the Kingdom
And the power and the glory
Forever.
Amen.

God, You're Real: First Encounter

The first time I knew God was real was as a little girl standing outside Canaan Baptist Church in Paterson, New Jersey. During this time, children were taught to be seen and not heard. The service had just ended, and the Pastor, Reverend Graham, stood outside the church's doors to shake the member's hands.

This day, he bent down and reached to shake my little hand. The sweat was still pouring down the sides of his face from preaching. He offered me a tremendous smile. At that moment, with the one-of-a-kind, grandiose robe he wore, I knew I mattered. I understood that God was aware of me and He could see me. I truly felt special that day.

Humanity has this longing to know

or understand God. We want to be seen and understood by our Heavenly Father. Trust today that our God sees us with an everlasting love.

There is no formula or method to make us instantly closer to God. We don't have to complicate how simple it is to connect with the one longing to connect and communicate with us.

Becoming One
1. When did you first know God was real?

2. How did you experience Him?

Face to Face

I met God again in the face and embrace of my grandmother. The glow that radiated from her face was mesmerizing. A presence of love flowed out of her and engulfed me in every hug.

Her confident, consistent smile and compassionate, fiery eyes spoke of a divine existence as much as the beautiful words that came out of her mouth. She talked about Jesus from morning until night. She clutched her Bible as if it were her closest friend. Her belly shook as she laughed or sang songs of adoration to God from the depths of her being.

In contrast, my parents had split up, and we ended up as a broken family living in New York City with little to no contact with extended family or friends. Living hundreds of miles away from my loving grandma in the city that never sleeps, I just couldn't find that same presence. I couldn't feel God or recognize Him anywhere.

Acknowledging the difference was painful.

No one I met talked about God. Walking down the streets with what seemed like millions of people or packed in a subway car full of strangers, I still couldn't see or feel Him.

The warmth I felt when visiting my grandma down south or outside Canaan Baptist Church was not there. That empty space in my life pushed me. For the first time, I decided to talk to God unscripted and unrehearsed. I told Him I believed He was real because I saw Him in my grandma's smile, hair, and how she carried herself. I told Him I could hear His love in her voice. That joyful exuberance and sparkle of the eye, the heartfelt praises that rang out as she sang songs about Him, testified in the court of the law of my heart. I was pretty sure God was real.

I just had to find Him.

Instinctively, I bowed my seven-year-old self to the ground and clasped my hands in front of my face. I asked God, "If you are real, take me out of this cold place, and I will believe in you and serve you for the rest of my life."

I believed that God loved the world and gave His only begotten Son, Jesus, to die for our sins and that He was crucified on the cross and that He rose from the dead, so I asked Him to take away my sins, give me eternal life, and to come into my heart.

Something in me changed, and although it was still dark and bleak outside, I couldn't seem to turn away. Hope and a glimmer of light shone on the inside.

I began a quest to know God and live by what I thought was suitable for Him to the best of my ability. I stopped cursing, fighting, and goofing off in class. I started to stand up for the underdog. I read the oversized Bible that was largely ignored in the kitchen closet. Although it made little sense to me, I kept on reading.

By age 11, we left Brooklyn, New York to live down south in a small town in North Carolina, which made us closer to my mom's family roots. A lot happened during that time, including my grandmother's passing. Middle school was difficult since we were always moving around from place to place. The one big Bible we owned had gotten lost in the move. There were no church services we attended.

My connection with God rested in a few songs that I would hear on the radio from time to time. I'm sure I still prayed, but I can't remember, as the time felt like silent years. I longed for God and just wanted to encounter Him face to face.

We become one with God by seeking Him with all our strength, mind, and soul. There is only one way–Jesus Christ. Through Him, we can become one with the Father and become one as the body of Christ.

We must start with God, His word, and who He says He is because so many things compete for our attention. Take the vast number of products to choose from, for instance. With so many choices, we wonder, how do I know the right choice?

We frantically read and search reviews to find other people's thoughts and perspectives on item(s) and conduct as much research as possible—sometimes on major and minor purchases.

In a world filled with religion and varying belief systems, it can be hard to choose because so many voices are trying to speak to us. Therefore, we must fine-tune our hearing and become more intimate with God as we learn to become one with Him. Jesus said, "My sheep will hear my voice, and the voice of a stranger they will not follow" (John 10:1-5, 27, NIV).

God of the universe desires a deep relationship with His creation–young and old. He has pursued us from the beginning, so the ball is in our court. Take the shot. Draw closer to Him.

Becoming One

1. How will you turn and come face to face with a God who wants to reveal Himself to you in an even greater, more personal way?

2. Still away for a moment, open your heart and mind, and focus on becoming one with Him.

One Lord, One Faith, One Baptism

There was a knock on the door and an unfamiliar face on the other side of the peephole. A bus full of lively youths was parked outside our tiny white house. A young teenage girl explained her church was having a special service for young people. She shared they had the transportation to get us to and from church if our parents gave us permission to attend.

There was such excitement and enthusiasm in the air my twin sister and I ran to ask our mom if we could head out that night with the strangers. All eyes were on mom, and silent prayers rang up to God, pleading to let her say yes. The moment she did, we ran out of the house and into the next phase of our spiritual journeys.

The preacher wore a crisp white shirt.

He held a microphone that he screamed into with such power and conviction. He talked about Jesus and asked us to decide to get baptized into Christ that night. We were allowed to show what had been done inside our hearts outwardly.

Those who said yes brought their towels and a change of clothes the next night. We entered one after another into that outdoor baptism pool (which likely served as a swimming pool at other times). Standing outside, beneath the stars, amidst the darkness, a light shone brightly in my heart and on my face. Coming out of the water was an indescribable feeling. I knew God was present.

What I know now but didn't know then was when I gave my heart to the Lord, I received John's baptism of repentance, and I was baptized into Christ. I was being made one with Him. However, I understood that submerging in the water symbolized Christ's death and burial for our sins. Coming out of the water symbolizes Jesus' resurrection from the dead. It was a glorious experience. That moment began my understanding of God's oneness—one Lord, one faith, one baptism.

Jesus states that I am the way, the

truth, and the life. No one comes to the Father except through me" (John 14:6, KJV).

Here, He is making a great claim that He is not one of many ways. Although God creates variety in many spheres, He is clear in the position of unity when it comes to being Lord, when it comes to faith, and when it comes to baptism. They all go hand in hand and all work together.

So, who is God?

He is the Father, the Son, and the Holy Spirit, and He is love.

Who is Jesus?

The scriptures establish that Jesus is God. In the beginning, was the Word (Jesus), and the Word (Jesus) was with God, and the Word (Jesus) was God (John 1:1).

One Lord. The Lord is God (Exodus 20:2-6). Jesus is the one mediator between God and men to unite us.

One faith. Unity in the faith and the knowledge of the Son of God is critical to our relationship with the Father and understanding His oneness. Faith involves believing beyond what we see and experience with our senses. Everything hinges on our belief in God and His Son, Jesus. Galatians 3:26-27 reads, "So in Christ Jesus, we are all children of God through faith."

One baptism. Galatians 3:27 reads, "You are baptized into our Lord and Savior Jesus Christ.

Notice the parallel–Lord to spirit, faith to the soul, and body to baptism.

Our Spirit is saved when we accept Jesus as Lord of our lives. Our mind, which is a part of our soul, must be renewed, and our body must surrender to the newness of life.

That day, deciding to get baptized furthered my journey of oneness with God.

Becoming One
1. Have you experienced baptism? What did it mean to you?

2. What has helped shape your ability to become one with God?

One Baptism

My family interactions give another example of variety. Sometimes we are in a silly mood and sit and talk about nothing but chicken. To us, it's hilarious to see how long we can carry on a conversation about chicken.

We talk about fried chicken, baked chicken, grilled chicken, chicken thighs, chicken legs, chicken wings, sesame chicken, lemon pepper chicken, BBQ chicken–you get the point.

Chicken is one meat, but it can be prepared in so many creative ways. Similarly, we can learn to appreciate the many creative ways God may want to use us individually and as a church body.

Churches also have their unique fingerprint and can get off course when they stop following God's vision. They may begin to follow the vision that the large or successful ministry has adopted. We don't all have to be alike or do everything the same way. God can use one person to minister in the streets and another to minister in Congress.

It doesn't make one person or gift greater or lesser than the other. Peter was called mainly to the Jews and Paul to the Gentiles.

We cannot take on a prejudiced mindset in the body of Christ about believers whose gifts are different from ours.

We must not have the mentality that we are the only ones doing Christianity "right."

The body of Christ is so much bigger than our local church or fellowshipping in our church buildings.

Dr. Tony Evans used an analogy once on unity. He talks about a football team. He describes having different positions for various players, but the players all have the same goal. It is the same end zone each player tries to bring the ball across.

We will be unified if we remember that we are on the same team.

Becoming One

1. Have you considered where God has uniquely placed you to be different from the crowd but still part of the crowd?

2. How do you show appreciation for how God uses others differently than you?

Baptism of the Holy Spirit

Being baptized in the Holy Spirit rocked my world and changed everything. God became alive in me. He was no longer way up in the sky where it took so long to get an answer. Now, it felt like He was inside me. I could hear Him speaking to me, and His voice changed my life forever.

I heard about people speaking in other languages or an unknown language called tongues. However, I wasn't around people who spoke in tongues enough to know if it was something they were making up or if their language was accurate.

I kept a stiff arm to the idea for quite some time since I didn't know anyone who spoke in those "so-called tongues," so I was very skeptical.

I was also apprehensive because I was taught that speaking in tongues only happened in the Bible days with the Apostles, and it no longer happened today because tongues had already ceased.

However, I wondered if tongues were a real thing God wanted me to have. I did not beat around the bush. I talked with God per usual, because the matter was serious to me.

If speaking in tongues was real, it would be up to Him to make it happen. I was emphatic about it not being *me* trying to speak some gibberish that I didn't understand, I was not going to repeat the words I heard others saying.

A year had already passed, and I was still trying to get the whole speaking in tongues thing underway–it just wasn't working. However, speaking in tounges happened in the scriptures, so I eventually reached the point of belief that tongues were real. From the east coast to the west coast, conferences, large and small gatherings, people praying, hollering with intensity, and spit flying over me, still no tongues.

I tried being a "good Christian," however, I eventually put tongues on the back burner and continued with my life. Graduating from college and getting married were my primary focuses.

Speaking in tongues remained on the back burner until my late twenties. Interestingly, around that time, I received a phone call from my twin sister, who had lived in California since our college graduation. I was filled with wonder as she told me she experienced speaking in tongues! Well, I've been knowing this girl from the womb. She's my bestie, wombmate, and "twin till the end."

I know her, and we are no-nonsense people, so I believed in the speaking of tongues when she told me. There was only one problem. I didn't know how to make it work.

Then I attended Bishop TD Jakes' "Woman Thou Art Loosed" conference with some family and friends in Atlanta, Georgia.

During one of the sessions, Darlene Bishop preached a message about desirability. She shared that whatever you desire when you pray, believe that you receive them, and you shall have them. Throughout the message, she let us know that at the end, she would allow us to pray and ask God for what we desired.

Then, I desired nothing more than the gift of speaking in tongues. Darlene Bishop prompted us to make our request. With all my heart and tears streaming down my face, I said, "Lord, more than anything, I desire the gift of speaking in tongues."

At that moment, I learned there is a difference between wanting and desiring something. I had wanted this gift for over a year, but the moment I desired it, everything changed.

A stillness came over me. My aunt saw something glorious happening inside me, and she embraced me. My tongue felt as if it were on fire; my belly rumbled as I began to hear unique sounds from my mouth. The tongues flowed freely.

Joy and jubilation filled my soul as I was baptized in the Holy Spirit with the evidence of speaking in tongues.

Becoming One
1. What are the desires of your heart?

2. How have your desires brought you closer
to God and created oneness with Him?

Prayer to Become One

Hallelujah! Glory to your name God!

Father, we thank you, praise you, and bless you today. Thank you for being faithful and true. You are a just God, and we are grateful that you bring us into unity and oneness with you.

God, we seek after you with all our heart, soul, might, and strength. You are wonderful. You are magnificent, there is none other like you. You created and framed the heavens and the Earth with your power, majesty, and wisdom. There is no one like our God.

We acknowledge you as King of

kings and Lord of lords, the double-breasted One. You are the One who knows the end from the beginning. You are faithful to a thousand generations, and we bless you Jehovah Jireh, the God who provides for us. You are Jehovah Shammah, The God who is there.

You are Jehovah Mekadesh, our Holy God who sanctifies. You are Jehovah Nissi, the God who is our Banner, and EL Elyon, the God of might and power. You are El Roi, The God who sees us, and we thank you and praise you for who you are. You are the great I AM, who is, and was, and is to come. Hallelujah to your name oh, God.

One Faith

One Faith

Prayer is essential in our union with God. That's what the numbers 1-1-1 that I kept noticing everywhere began to symbolize to me—the need to become one with God through prayer. Life apart from prayer is a disconnection from God. It's a disconnection from the True Vine, Jesus, who is the word of God. We must understand the tenants of prayer and cultivate a lifestyle of prayer that supports the direction of God's call.

<u>Our Prayer</u>

Our Father,
who art in heaven,
hallowed be thy name;
thy kingdom come;
thy will be done

on earth as it is in heaven.
Give us this day our daily bread;
and forgive us our trespasses
as we forgive those who trespass against us;
and lead us not into temptation,
but deliver us from evil.
For thine is the Kingdom
And the power and the glory
Forever.
Amen.

Teaching on Prayer

I was affectionately referred to as the resident elder on the leadership team of the women's ministry at my local church. While having a virtual book club discussion, the conversation took an interesting twist.

We began to talk about praying publicly and why so few do it and are intimidated by it. I made a few comments about the need for training in this area.

Unbeknownst to me, our Senior Pastor brought his wife, our host pastor, dinner at that very moment and overheard my comments.

He interjected to inform us that I would be teaching about prayer for two Thursday night bible studies. Of course, my prayer life kicked in. The anointing of "shut up" came over me, forbidding me from talking myself out of the assignment. I honestly did not see it coming.

At that moment, God started to download the message–God wanted us to have His heart, the heart of the Master.

God impressed upon me that He wanted my heart and the heart of the children to turn to the Father.

Prayer gives a fresh perspective. I heard Deborah Pegues, guest speaker of Focus on the Family, share a powerful acronym for prayer:

P-Pause and focus on God; give your undivided attention.
R-Reverence. Don't bring God down to our level; nothing is too hard for God.
A-Ask for guidance and wisdom.
Y-Yield to God's word and His will, not yours.

P-Prioritize every aspect of life.
E-Expect less from people and more from God.
A-Acknowledge God in everything.
C-Cultivate contentment.

E-Eliminate sin.

Source: Deborah Pegues, Focus on the Family.
Becoming One

1. How do you cultivate your prayer life?

2. Meditate on the scriptures below about prayer. What does the Father download to you?

Matthew 6:5-8
Hebrews 4:16
1 Thessalonians 5:16-18
Philippians 4:6-7

The Power of YOUR Prayers

It was the 11th day of the first month. My body lay prostrate on my living room floor; in a few hours, it would be the first time I'd deliver a message to a group of women at my church.

God started to rearrange the message I labored over and prepared. He said, "Tell them they don't know how powerful their prayers are."

Instantly, I understood. God was showing me the power of our prayers, and we must pray like our life depends on it because it does.

The power of OUR prayers can and does save lives. It changes outcomes, and it changes us.

We see in Matthew 6:5, that Jesus expects us to pray. He says, "when you pray…"

He not only expects us to pray but commands us to pray without ceasing (1 Thessalonians 5:16-18) and identifies that His house shall be called a house of prayer (Matthew 21:12-14).

Becoming One
1. How can you enhance your prayer life?

2. How has prayer changed something in your life or the life of someone you've covered in prayer?

A Rainbow
of Prayers

While prayer is a vast topic, it's essential that we know about prayer and the types of prayers because prayer accomplishes so much. It makes tremendous power available to us. Therefore, it is essential in our lives at home, at church, in business and the like. Again, Jesus said, "My house shall be called a house of prayer" (Matthew 21:13).

Therefore, prayer is crucial to the life of the believer. There are several types of prayer to recognize but the types of prayer, although distinguished, usually are not just cut and dry. At any given moment, the different types of prayer can overlap like a rainbow, as they are all connected. At times, some colors in the rainbow may stand out more than others, and the same is true when it comes to the types of prayer. Likewise, just as the colors of the rainbow can't be separated, the same is true with various types of prayer.

When I learned there were different types of prayers, I decided to work at knowing all of them and more importantly, how to incorporate the different types of prayers as an arsenal for real life situations and circumstances. Let's explore a few of the type of prayers available to us.

The Prayer of Thanksgiving

The prayer of thanksgiving is my favorite. It seems to be the access into the presence of God. When I thank God for who He is and what He has done, my heart is filled with gratitude.

Negative things, the trials of life, misunderstandings, and anything else seem to fade into the background. It's like a chain reaction when I begin to thank God, bringing joy and the realization that He is near. Psalms 100:4 tells us to "enter into His gates with thanksgiving and come into His courts with praise."

The Prayer of Consecration

Consecration prayers sacredly set

something or someone apart unto God. Every ordination or baby dedication usually includes a prayer of consecration. We can consecrate our lives, our possessions, and professions by setting them apart as sacred unto God.

The Prayer of Intercession

Intercession is simply praying to God on behalf of another. Anytime we pray for our spouse, children, family, members of the community, or church, we engage in intercessory prayer.

The Prayer of Petition

Petition is another type of prayer involving a written request to God.

An example of a prayer of petition was when we were believing God for a house. God put it in my heart to be very specific about the house. Although we had been praying for a house for a while, I almost got the sense that God was not going to bring a house unless we could articulate what was really desired. Writing out the list and then typing it became the launch pad for our faith. Seeing our request to God helped weed out the houses we would have settled for previously. Sure enough, nothing short of what we thought was a miracle happened. Within months, we were actually living in our five bedroom, three and a half bath home, in a great neighborhood, at a very good price.

It's the same prayer tactic I used to find my husband years earlier.

Right now, I am asking God for every reader to experience tremendous growth in their prayer life and a deeper relationship with Him as we become one with Him. Personal petition prayers can be wonderful because later there is proof that God answered the specific request.

This point may sound like a contradiction, but petition prayers do not technically have to be written. The Bible says my tongue is as the pen of a ready writer. (Psalms 45:1) Therefore we can speak out petitions and they are still recorded in the atmosphere.

However, I strongly recommend writing it out—there's something about a written vision that is spoken out that seems to have a more powerful impact.

The Prayer of Supplication

Supplication at its root is a request involving simple humility.

There are convenient stores called 7-eleven. Years ago, the stores were very popular because other convenient stores had routine, confined hours. 7-eleven had extended hours, opening early and closing late, and became synonymous with "all the time."

It's the prayer I like to keep in my front pocket. All throughout the day, we can pray to God asking Him to change us and make us more like Him. We can ask Him for understanding for the things going on around us and in us. We can ask Him to help us surrender to His will in our decision making and to grow our grace, love, and compassion for others. The key thing to remember is to come to God with a humble heart because we recognize that we are asking for help from the Creator of the universe.

When you couldn't reach anyone else, you could reach 7- eleven. Matthew 7:11 is what I call the open heaven scripture because it allows us to reach God at any time. It states, "Ask and it will be given to you; seek and you will find; knock and the door will be opened to you."

Similarly, Jeremiah 33:3 reads, "call to me and I will answer you and tell you great and unsearchable things you do not know."

Supplication prayers always amazes me because God is willing to get into the details and nitty gritty of our lives. He said He would never leave nor forsake us, and He is not a man that He should lie. So, we really can call on Him and know He's there. We really can ask, and God will give us anything we ask for according to His will. We really can knock and have doors open up for us. When we seek, we really do find.

Prayer is a vast subject with different types of ways to engage with the Father, but we must make it essential in our lives, at home, church, business, and wherever we are. While praying, know that we can cry out to God, and He hears and answers us.

Becoming One
1. What type of prayer do you most often

pray?

2. How can you begin incorporating other prayer types into your prayer time?

Travailing Prayers

It's been my experience that travailing prayer is the least understood type of prayer. Transparently, I don't fully understand it, but I have experienced it and can share from my experiences. *However, the scriptures trump any experience we may have as individuals.*

When we experience something that someone else may not have experienced, it becomes a part of our reality. For example, I have physically given birth to five children. Each birthing was similar but also a bit different. For me to explain to my husband, who was present at every delivery, what I truly experienced, and expect him to understand what giving birth to a baby is really like would be unfair. He was there but only as a very close and present spectator.

Meanwhile, I was in the game. I was the only one who could give birth to those babies, there was work, sweating, and some groaning involved when the contractions hit. When the intensity rose, I had to push. In comparison to everyone else in the room, I wasn't as calm or casual. The doctor, nurse, and my husband all looked respectable, but I couldn't deliver the baby fully clothed. Something wonderful and full of life had been growing inside me for months, and the time had come to deliver. I had to travail in birth until the child was born.

Travailing prayer also has to do with giving birth. However, travailing prayer is spiritual. Paul says in Galatians 4:19-20, "My little children, of whom I travail in birth again until Christ be formed in you" (KJV).

Those who yield themselves to the Holy Spirit can find themselves travailing in prayer.

Depending on how the Holy Spirit is moving a person, it can involve strong crying, weeping, or groaning. The intensity can be very real, and the levels of intensity can also vary. Travailing prayer can be expressed as a sinking feeling in the gut, an intense workout, or a feeling of giving natural birth. Just like we can't orchestrate a natural birth, we cannot orchestrate a spiritual birth—as it is the work of the Spirit of God.

This level of birthing can take place because God wants to bring new life. Likewise, "the Spirit also helpeth our infirmities: for we know not what we should pray for as we ought: but the Spirit Himself maketh intercession for us with groanings which cannot be uttered" (Romans 8:26).

Travailing prayer happens when God wants to birth something, He's grieved about something, or something grievous is about to take place. It's important to pray these burdens through. It could be the difference between death and life, mercy and judgment.

Jesus is also found praying and travailing, "who in the days of his flesh, when he had offered up prayers and supplications with strong crying and tears unto him that was able to save him from death and was heard in that he feared;" (Hebrews 5:7).

Travail has the power to transform us into Christlikeness. The whole earth is in a travail for the children of God to be who

God has called us to be (Romans 8:22-23).

Becoming One

1. Have you ever experienced a travailing prayer?

2. Are you willing to allow the Holy Spirit to travail in prayer through you?

Keys to the Kingdom: What the Bible Says about Travailing Prayer by Betty Miller is a great article on the subject at Bibleresources.org.

The Prayer of Faith and Agreement

The prayer of agreement requires at least one other person, whereas the prayer of faith does not. However, they both, require faith.

Faith is simply believing in God and trusting Him for a desired outcome. The prayer of faith has a supernatural component to it. It requires that God intervenes beyond our human capabilities.

During a time when I was on maternity leave, Maurice worked odd jobs. With six kids at the time, it just wasn't enough. We had gotten seriously behind on everything and needed thousands of dollars by the end of the week! We didn't know who we could ask for help or even how to ask for help. My thought was *ONLY GOD CAN HELP US!*

Well, Maurice must have been thinking the same thing.

He grabbed my hands and said, "We're going to believe God for this money to come in."

I was speechless and just nodded my head. He began to pray about the specific dollar amount that we needed. I agreed with everything He prayed. If you know the God I serve, you know what happened next. By the end of the week, we had more money than we needed! *Glory to God in the highest!*

Turns out, Maurice ran into an old friend who desperately needed referrals. Well, Maurice negotiated for $100 per referral and brought that man so much business that week it was incredible! We can believe God when it looks impossible, that's the prayer of faith. It has the power to heal and save.

No matter how difficult or hopeless your situation looks, there is a God ready, willing, and able to help you if you believe. Sometimes, we have to build ourselves up on our most holy faith. Sometimes, we have to call for the Elders so the prayer of faith can heal us.

When two or more come together, God is in the midst. If they agree on any point, God says he will do what they have asked. His words are true and can be applied in our lives.

Becoming One
1. Who agrees with you during prayer? Write the name of your prayer partner.

2. What will you believe God for that is outside of your human abilities to make happen?

The Prayer Agenda

Awakened by the Holy Spirit's voice, in the middle of the night, the Holy Spirit asked me, "Will you write out a prayer agenda?"

Immediately, I grabbed my paper and pen and began to write out an agenda for prayer.

Today, I'm still looking for the paper I scribbled on that night and have since learned my lesson and become better at writing important things down in a place I will remember and keep safe.

While some thoughts that the Holy Spirit shared with me are clear, others are blurred.

I didn't treat the word of the Lord as precious as it was and some words remained lost over the years, and for that, I am truly repentant.

Sometimes the Lord first gives us something, and it is so clear that He is speaking.

Then with the passage of time and the cares of life, we begin to question what we were once certain about.

That's why I like the pen. If I can get what the Holy Spirit shares with me on paper while it's fresh, it becomes a document or a notarized letter that I can refer to when I need proof.

Transparently, there are times when hearing isn't as clear, and we begin to wonder if we are speaking or if it is the Lord speaking within us.

Know God's voice and when He's leading and calling you to do something for Him to glorify His kingdom. Pay attention to and take seriously the things He downloads in prayer or when you're awakened in the middle of the night.

I was a young, expectant mother when God gave me the word about crafting a prayer agenda. I was a literal house of prayer. There was no place set aside in my home to pray, and there was no set prayer time.

However, I was a living, breathing prayer machine. I constantly prayed and talked to the Lord.

God's sheep hear His voice. Listen for His voice and take it seriously. Hold true to what He says and take care of His word.

Becoming One

1. What agenda is God sharing with you?

2. How will you protect what God has shared with you?

Fasting

Fasting is another spiritual tool that brings us to oneness with God and enhances our prayers.

However, the motive for fasting has to be pure and for spiritual reasons in order to be effective. I have experienced the supernatural power of God surrounding a fast, and I have experienced seemingly nothing surrounding a fast. The true motive driving the fast is key to the results gained.

If we sense that God wants us to fast and we comply, we will likely see tremendous spiritual results.

The motive behind fasting can't be to lose weight or to try and twist God's arm into getting our desires. The real purpose of a fast is to help our outward physical senses give way to our inner spiritual being.

Fasting helps us humble ourselves and provides us with the mindset needed to align with God's will. Fasting humbles our soul (Psalms 35:13).

Just as there are different types of prayer, there are different types of fasting.

Fasting can produce many excellent outcomes, especially when paired with prayer.

It can cause breakthroughs in habits, situations, and circumstances that otherwise were not changing.

Scriptures also pinpoint prayer and fasting as means to rid unbelief, "this kind [of unbelief or stronghold] comes out only by prayer and fasting" (Matthew 17:21).

Fasting can be a direct correlation to increased and strengthened faith.

Satan doesn't want us to know how powerful fasting is when it's coupled with prayer.

Spend time meditating on the scriptures to hear God during your fast.

Becoming One

1. What will you choose to surrender during your time of fasting?

2. How did God move for you during your time of fasting?

God's Chosen Fast

God has chosen a fast for us!

The fast that He chooses is that we stop pointing the finger at others in judgment. According to Isaiah 58, His fast requires us to look out for the poor, needy, and homeless, and feed and clothe them. His fast also requires that we free those who are oppressed, break bondages off people, and release the wicked traps that hold people.

Fasting can help shift our mindset from autonomy to oneness. Those who live as stand-alone Christians can come out of isolation. Isolation is a sure way to get off track because there is no accountability, which has the potential to lead to doing whatever we think is right. We can think something is right, but that very thing can lead us to death.

Sometimes were fasting because we want to get our way, but fasting can actually bring us to a place of spiritual strength to deny what we want in favor of wanting what God wants for us. Fasting can bring us to a place where we can say not my will, but your will be done God.

The most important thing to know about fasting is that it must be done with the right motive and for spiritual reasons.

Fasting helps to sharpen our spiritual senses. It can give us divine access, produce supernatural power, breakthroughs and deliverance. With fasting, we get greater clarity, and it is an enhancement to our prayer time.

Becoming One

1. What are the most important benefits of fasting to you?

2. Have you experienced a breakthrough in life due to fasting?

Living Waters

I had a dream that our pastor was giving a word of wisdom to an Elder and prayer leader in the church. He called her by name, saying, "it takes living waters to write a book."

There was more to the dream, and I shared it with her. She was very encouraged but said, "I don't know about the book part."

The interesting thing was that I could hear the books, subjects, and chapters all in the conversation we had on the phone, but she didn't think so.

God has many books to be written, they may not all be for the entire world, but they could be for your family.

The Bible says we are "epistles to be

read of men" (2 Corinthians 3:23).

What if we take that scripture literally?

If so, that means people read our lives just as a person would read a book.

What if we made things a little easier and gave them an actual book to see further into the goodness of God in our lives?

How powerful would it be if we all took the time to write out our personal testimonies?

How could our lives be enhanced by writing down the dreams we receive?

Could God have shown you some business idea, vision, or dream of what is to come?

A lot of time can pass before a dream or prophecy comes to pass, fret not. God will perform what He promises.

Becoming One
1. Have you taken the time to write out your testimony? If so, what is your testimony?

2. Do you keep a journal by your bed to record the dreams you feel that God is giving you?

Taming the
Sinful Nature

Everybody wants to be loved. As a man, Jesus was no different, He wanted to be well-liked and received, but He was rejected. If He catered to people, He would not be doing God's will.

If we cater to people, we can't be the servants of Christ (Galatians 1:10).

Christ wants us to pick up our cross and follow Him. Our sinful, flesh nature is always working to oppose this work in us.

In my life, picking up my cross means I can't win every argument, I can't have the last word, I can't always be right even when I think I'm right, I have to give my right away to pursue peace.

Coming from a very loud and boisterous family, I have a tendency to want to fight and defend myself and make sure that my voice is also heard.

I haven't always been saved, and I have to pull on grace from the Holy Ghost, so I don't offend in word or deed.

We can only yield in this way through prayer and fasting. Fasting helps to tame the sinful carnal nature. John 12:24 states, "unless wheat falls into the ground and dies, it abides alone. But if it dies, it bears fruit."

Dying gives birth. Allow your flesh to die to the sinful nature through prayer and fasting.

Becoming One
1. What does picking up your cross look like in your life?

2. What aspects of your life should die through prayer and fasting?

Write the Vision

I was so lonely in college, watching couples hold hands and talk about their relationships. I prayed, "Lord, will I ever meet the man of my dreams?"

It's important to know that if we are one and abide in Him, we can ask for anything according to His will in His name and He gives us the desires of our hearts (1 John 5:15-15, John 14:13-14, John 15:7, Proverbs 37:4).

I recalled writing a list at 14 years old that identified everything I wanted.

1. He must be a virgin.
2. He must love God before knowing me.
3. He must have potential.

4. He must love me for me.

There were other factors, but those were the deal breakers!

My list wasn't outward. Instead, it was an inward list dealing with the character and internal makeup. I knew God had my list.

At the time, our college girlfriend, Devonda, asked my sister and me to go on a triple date with her. She already had her guy picked and the date set. We had to secure our dates in the next couple of weeks.

My sister had her date in record time. I, on the other hand, was a nervous wreck.

How could a girl ask a guy out?

The pressure was on, and they made it clear that I was leaving mid-week service with a date for Friday night. We three stood at the back of the church, panning the room for a date. "What about him, or him, or him, or him?" they tag-teamed suggested.

I kept looking. Then, my twin asked, "What about him?"

I had previously met him at a Bible

study on campus and had seen him at my dorm. Hmmm? Ok, I'll ask him as soon as I take a few more deep breaths and ask God for the courage and the words. I stuttered and stammered, but I finally got the question out.

"I would love to," Maurice responded. I ran back to my girls with the thumbs up, and we laughed and giggled our way out of the sanctuary.

Is there something specific you are believing God for? Have you written it down?

God honors what we believe and record. Habakkuk 2:2 states, "write the vision and make it plain." Write your vision and watch God work in your favor.

Becoming One
1. What do you believe God for at this stage of life?

2. What vision or desire do you need to write and put before the Lord?

Prayer to Become One

Dear heavenly Father,

You are a great and awesome God, the Alpha and Omega, the beginning and the end, the all-seeing and all-knowing God.

Thank you for who you have been in our lives and for making us partakers of your divine nature. Thank you for your precious Holy Spirit that you have given as a down payment of our inheritance and promises from you.

Thank you for your word that illuminate our hearts and transforms our minds. We desire to serve you and be united with you.

Father God, help your children unite in you. Let us throw away everything that divides and alienates us from the life and love of God. Bring us into tender fellowship with each other. You said they would know that we are your children, your disciples by our love.

Let love bind us, let love motivate and inspire us. Thank you for tender mercy and compassion flowing through your church, the bride of Christ. Make us a loving people that are full of the fruits of your spirit. We want to be full of peace, love, joy, patience, goodness, kindness, faithfulness, gentleness, and self-control. Father God, you desire for us to be one, help us to do those things that please you.

We drive fear, intimidation, and condemnation out of your body. We pray that the bride of Christ makes herself ready, in Jesus' name. Amen.

One Body

One Body

Unity in the body of Christ is critical for us to ensure the message of Christ is broadcast through the earth. We are the hands and feet of Jesus, and it is our job to support each other and those looking to grow in relationship with the Father. "For just as the body is one and has many members, and all the members of the body, though many, are one body, so it is with Christ. For in one Spirit, we were all baptized into one body— Jews or Greeks, slaves or free—and all were made to drink of one Spirit" (1 Corinthians 12:12-13).

Our Prayer

Our Father,
who art in heaven,
hallowed be thy name;

thy kingdom come;
thy will be done
on earth as it is in heaven.
Give us this day our daily bread;
and forgive us our trespasses
as we forgive those who trespass against us;
and lead us not into temptation,
but deliver us from evil.
For thine is the Kingdom
And the power and the glory
Forever.
Amen.

We Are Many;
We Are One

It was my sixth-grade graduation. Parents and teachers filled the seats in the auditorium.

All the sixth graders sang, "We are many, we are one, brothers and sisters wherever you're from, we all dance to a different drum. We are many, but we are one," from the top of our lungs.

We exhaled with our hearts pounding furiously as we finished Up with People's last lines in the song. We were so excited, grinning from ear to ear. I labored to take in more breaths. Up and down, my chest went, yet I had the biggest smile on my face.

It was the warmest feeling like the sun gently shining down. The audience's thunderous claps and cheers inflated my inner confidence and happy buttons like a cake on the rise.

Ephesians 4:11-16 reads:
So, Christ himself gave the apostles, the prophets, the evangelists, the pastors, and teachers to equip his people for works of service so that the body of Christ may be built until we all reach unity in the faith and the knowledge of the Son of God and become mature, attaining to the whole measure of the fullness of Christ.

Then we will no longer be infants, tossed back and forth by the waves, and blown here and there by every wind of teaching and by the cunning and craftiness of people in their deceitful scheming. Instead, speaking the truth in love, we will grow to become in every respect the mature body of Him who is the head, that is, Christ. From Him, the whole body is joined and held together by every supporting ligament, grows, and builds itself up in love as each part does its work.

Like the message of that song, this passage also reminds me that although we as a people are many and different, we are one race.

We are the human race. No matter where we come from, we're all brothers and sisters, and we can grow together as one.

Becoming One
1. How do you practice becoming one with others?

2. How do you purpose to become one with God?

Diversity of Operations

Sometimes, I participate in prayer groups. Once, I recall everyone (*except me)* knew I was the one with "the word from the Lord."

There was an older lady who looked at me with such annoyance. She communicated nonverbally, and the message was, will you just spit it out already?

Feeling embarrassed in that moment, I thought I should know something I just didn't know.

Wouldn't you know it? Several minutes later, I felt bubbling in my gut, so I cooperated and began speaking in what's referred to in the Bible as tongues.

Biblical tongues are simply a gift of language that God gifts anyone who sincerely desires it.

After I finally got the message out, another person interpreted the message, and we were all thrilled and blessed. However, these were very uncomfortable interactions for me because my brain wasn't making sense of them, and it seemed that I had been looked to for an interpretation I didn't seem to have.

Hindsight is often 20-20.

Looking back, I wish I had spent more time with the Lord to let Him explain things to me. Instead, I ran. I did not like putting myself out there. I wondered if I'd given too much leeway to my flesh, and I couldn't help but wonder what others thought.

I tried to hide, be quiet, and draw as little attention to myself as possible. After all, I wanted to be respected and appreciated just like anyone else.

Much later, I wonder what would have happened if I hadn't been a stand-alone Christian. I tried to ask for help once, but I didn't get the help that I asked for and felt ignored.

I can't help but think about what my life, my family's life, and all the people I encounter would be like if I had been fearless, trusted God, and kept seeking wise counsel until I found it.

What opportunities did I miss where I could have made an impact?

How might God have used me if I had developed this gift?

So, here I am, years later, just beginning this journey to understand. Think of yourself the way God thinks about you! That type of thinking will grant you all the confidence needed to operate in your uniquely designed gift.

Becoming One
1. In what area(s) are you running away from God?

2. How does God want to use you, but you are uncomfortable because you don't know how people will react?

No More Division

During high school, my mom had an encounter with God. That encounter changed everything–we became members of a local church.

One Sunday morning, right over the pulpit, the pastor told my twin and me to come and sing with the choir. Our new seats were right behind the pulpit. We even joined a community choir.

The pastor rattled off scripture after scripture without looking at His notes. Those familiar scriptures, coupled with his analogies and explanations, filled in some of the long-standing questions I wondered about. Understanding the scriptures brought me closer to God. It made Him more real to me.

However, now my questions emerged from observations. For example, why was the church divided?

People on the left side of the church gave testimonies during testimony service, said Amen, and sat in the front rows. The people on the right side of the church sat with blank stares or folded arms. They also sat towards the back of the church. Not clearly knowing what their actions meant, there were clear signs of disunity.

There are mindset shifts and perspectives that we can develop to assist us in resisting division and help us to become more unified.

Do you identify yourself by a particular group of people, or do you see yourself as part of all humanity?
The Bible teaches us to "avoid genealogies, foolish questions and debates knowing that they cause and bring about strife" (Titus 3:9).

Why would God instruct us to avoid genealogies, the "line of descent traced continuously from an ancestor?"

When others try to divide us through

race, economic status, education, or background, we must be mindful of the bigger picture.

God created us to be a part of His family, and we have the right to choose whether to accept or reject Him. We decide if we will accept or reject each other.

Holding on too firmly to our family tree may cause us to become bitter or feel superior to others. Genealogies can bring about strife with its anger, bitterness, and conflict. Simply put, the emphasis should not be placed on our backgrounds because doing so brings a tendency and opportunity for ill will, disputes, disharmony, hostility, and the like.

Becoming One

1. Do you identify yourself with a particular group of people or see yourself as part of all humanity? Explain.

2. Why would God instruct us to avoid genealogies, the "line of descent traced continuously from an ancestor?"

Leaning on the Body

In difficult times or during testing and trials, it's important to remember that we are part of a body.

Have you ever been scratched and perhaps began to bleed, but didn't realize it immediately?

After a while, you might have felt some slight pain from or near the injured area. As you search for where the pain is coming from, you notice the small cut and begin to take steps to heal.

Some will use an antiseptic, while others use a band-aid. Pain is the body's way of asking for help.

Similarly, as believers, we must be

willing to signal to the body of believers when we need help.

Certainly, a blow to the head, heart, or any vital organ will get immediate attention, while cuts, scrapes, and bruises aren't always felt or treated the moment they happen. We must become more aware of what's going on within our body and not be ashamed when we need support or healing from the Father or those in the body of Christ.

Becoming One
1. What areas of your life need healing?

2. How can you give those areas the attention they deserve, and who in the body of Christ might be able to support you?

Made in His Image

Genesis 1: 26 reads, "Let us make man in our image, after our likeness: and let them have dominion over the fish of the sea, and over the fowl of the air, and over the cattle, and over all the earth, and over every creeping thing that creepeth upon the earth."

Here, God introduces Himself as the one who creates, moves, and speaks. Likewise, we can create, move, and speak due to being made in God's image.

Although these are three ways we can function, we are still one person. As physical beings operating under physical law, our movements are limited to our whereabouts.

God, however, has no such restriction unless He chooses, much like Jesus did when

He came to live in a body.

Know today that you are made in God's image; nothing can stop you.

Becoming One
1. How do you see God's likeness reflected in your life?

2. How do you experience God's limitless power?

Partakers

We are partakers of His divine nature. According to Merriam-Webster, to partake means "to join in or experience something along with others: to have a portion (as of food or drink) and to possess or share a certain nature or attribute."

As Believers, we experience God's divine nature together–which is why communion is so important. During that time, we share Christ's death by symbolically eating His body and drinking His blood. This act means we are embracing that Jesus' body was crucified for us, and His blood was shed to save our eternal souls.

Finally, we possess the nature of God.

From the beginning, Satan has tried

to convince man that He is not yet like God. Man needs something more and must work or do something to obtain this divine nature. The truth is the first man, Adam, was already like God.

He was made in God's image and His likeness. 2 Corinthians 3:18 NKJV reads, "But we all, with unveiled face, beholding as in a mirror the glory of the Lord, are being transformed into the same image from glory to glory, just as by the Spirit of the Lord."

When we unite with Christ, we become more and more like Him.

Becoming One
1. How are you uniting with Christ?

2. How often do you commune with God?

Unity and Oneness

God's ability and capabilities far exceed all of humanity. He says we will only know in part while we live on earth (1 Corinthians 13:9 NLT).

Therefore, our knowledge is partial and incomplete, and even the gift of prophecy reveals only part of the whole picture. We must accept that God's superiority allows Him to be God the Father, Son, and Holy Spirit all at once.

According to 1 John 5:7, "There are three that bear witness in heaven: the Father, the Word, and the Holy Spirit; and these three are one."

Then, we see that "the Lord shall be King over all the earth. On that day, it shall be— 'The Lord is ONE,' And His name is ONE" (Zechariah 14:9, NKJV).

Scripture references the concept of God being one. It is the recurring idea that God divinely orchestrated and ordained the principle of unity and oneness.

Becoming One
1. How do you see God's oneness portrayed in scripture and in your life?

2. Why are unity and oneness with God critical to your relationship with Him?

Covenants

My definition of covenant is God binding Himself to an oath or promise for the benefit of mankind.

Marriage is a covenant. It's God's idea. There was a time earlier in my marriage that I did not want to be married anymore because it was too hard, and I wanted out. I overheard Maurice unconsciously mumbling to himself that he had married the wrong person. Here he was thinking that I was the problem, and there I was thinking he was the problem.

Well, I began to delve into scripture looking for a way out of our marriage that I could no longer envision being in for the rest of my life. To my disappointment at the time, there was no way out. He wasn't an abusive husband, and he hadn't committed adultery. I was stuck. In my heart, I knew that if I walked out of the marriage, I was really walking out on God. I was breaking His covenant and what I understood from the Bible and deciding that I was going to live life on my terms.

Well, I knew that God loved me and didn't want me to be miserable the rest of my life and if He was calling me to stay married, He had to have a better way. With the realization that I could not just walk out due to the charge to honor God and the covenant vow, I knew that I had to find His way of doing marriage. I begin to educate myself on what it would take to have a successful marriage. I read book, after book, after book, and my mind began to expand. I began to understand why my husband acted the way he did, and why I acted the way I acted. It became clear, we both had a lot of growing up and changing to do.

I wouldn't worry about his stuff as much because, to my amazement, my list of things to change was quite lengthy, and seeing my list gave me a more graceful attitude towards my husband. My perspective changed. Instead of being critical, I became more appreciative. Our marriage continued to get better and better. Honoring God and His covenant saved our marriage.

God created man but everything in man's heart was evil, so God was sorry that He made man. He destroyed all the evil and only let righteous Noah and his family survive the flood. When the earth dried, Noah made a sacrifice to God, it moved God so much that He made a covenant with mankind that He would never destroy all living things by flooding the earth. The symbol of His covenant was the rainbow in the sky.

Jesus came with a new covenant, His blood was the sacrifice, and the new covenant is that God writes His laws upon our hearts, that He will be our God, and we will be His people. Through accepting God's promise, His new covenant, we become one with Him.

Becoming One
1. Have you made a promise or an agreement that you later wanted to get out of?

2. How will you respond to the promises God has made to you by way of covenant?

One in Him

Colossians 3:15 reads, "Let the peace of Christ rule in your hearts since you were called to peace as members of one body. And be thankful."

So many denominations exist, and often each is based on a particular scripture or set of scriptures. However, the problem comes when our denominations begin to take on a mindset of "separation" instead of the unity found in Christ.

Paul was called to the Gentiles, and Peter was called to the Jews, but it was all for the same purpose of winning souls to Christ.

Therefore, we must remember that Jesus' whole work was to bring us together and make us one with the Father. He came to save the lost; if we keep His focus, we will be one in Him.

Jesus said it best in Matthew 12:30, "Anyone who is not with me is against me. Anyone who does not gather sheep with me scatters them."

Let's practice being one in Him.

Becoming One
1. How do you become one with the Father?

2. Have you seen or experienced disunity amongst denominations?

Prayer to Become One

Father, thank you that you are emboldening us and perfecting the things that concern us. You're moving into our future and causing us to walk agreeable to your will.

You know the plans that you have for us Lord God and you are causing us to walk towards you and the light that you have given us.

The glory of the Lord is upon us, our hearts are on fire for you Lord God, and you are breathing upon, cleansing, and purifying us. Your spirit captivates, draws, teaches, and guides us. Your will is being accomplished in this Earth through us.

You're going into the deep places, the recesses of our hearts and of our minds and you're causing us to be unified with you, Father in thought, word, and action. We are functioning as a body, the way you intended us to function.

We are staying in step and in tune with you. We seek your voice Father God, and we are diligently listening to and obeying your words. God, your word transform our hearts and our mind. You remove every schism and everything that is not beneficial, healthy, or needful for the body. You are moving it away from us and causing us to work in harmony with one another.

You're causing us to have strength in our inner being. You revive and quicken our weakest areas, making us strong. You renew our strength as we call out to you.

We accomplish everything you have laid out for us to accomplish in this life. You feed us daily and daily load us up with benefits. Your words nourish us and cause life to flow through us. You send forth your word and it heals and delivers us. Your power, grace, and anointing are present to heal and restore us. In Jesus' name, Amen.

One Enemy

One Enemy

Satan is subtle and known as the angel of light. In other words, he pretends to be on the side of good, but he is evil. Often the enemy comes as though he is our friend and has our best interest at heart. All the while, he has schemed and planned for our demise. "Yea, my own familiar friend, in whom I trusted, which did eat of my bread, has lifted his heel against me" (Psalm 41:9).

Our Prayer

Our Father,
who art in heaven,
hallowed be thy name;
thy kingdom come;
thy will be done
on earth as it is in heaven.
Give us this day our daily bread;

**and forgive us our trespasses
as we forgive those who trespass against
us;
and lead us not into temptation,
but deliver us from evil.**
For thine is the Kingdom
And the power and the glory
Forever.
Amen.

The Subtle Enemy

When it comes to the most famous betrayal, we often think of Judas. Jesus asked him, "Friend, do you betray me with a kiss?"

Judas and Jesus went from town-to-town ministering together. Judas got to hear the messages of Jesus firsthand. He was able to ask him questions when the crowds went away. They shared intimate spaces.

Psalm 41:9 states, "Yea, my own familiar friend, in whom I trusted, which did eat of my bread, has lifted his heel against me."

What causes close friends to betray?

What causes a spouse to turn on their partner?

Often the enemy comes as though he is our friend, on our side, and has our best interest at heart. All the while, he has schemed and planned our demise.

Don't forget this vital point: Satan entered Judas.

Many times, when someone close to us begins to act differently, we wonder why in the world they would act like, say, or do that."

Sometimes we ask those questions of ourselves. Could we have, in some way, let the thoughts and deception of the enemy influence us?

We must be valiant and remain alert of the enemy and his tactics. We cannot allow or afford to believe Satan's lies.

Becoming One
1. Has the enemy deceived or influenced you? If so, how?

2. What is your plan to stand against Satan?

Liar

Remember when Peter and Jesus spoke, and Peter tried to tell Jesus he wouldn't have to die?

Jesus knew those words were untrue, as He came to earth to die for the sins of the world. Peter may have been looking out for himself.

Jesus turned and said to Peter, "Get behind Me, Satan! You are a stumbling block to Me; for you are not setting your mind on things of God, but on things of man" (Matthew 16:23, AMP).

Similarly, do you find it ironic that this same Peter later asks Ananias a very revealing question? "Ananias, why has Satan filled your heart?" (Acts 5:3, NIV).

Peter goes on to ask Ananias, which gives us the insight that Ananias could have made a different decision. He could have resisted the schemes of Satan instead of letting him fill his heart with lies.

Whose idea was it to keep back part of the money from the house he sold and gave to the apostles while at the same time pretending it was the total amount so he could appear that his giving was directed by the Holy Spirit, like the other believers.

These plans from the enemy were very subtle and tricky. They looked like they would work, but they were exposed to the revelation that the Spirit of God brings.

Ananias and his wife, who also lied and agreed with Satan's plan, both fell dead and did not get away with their lies.

The subtle enemy may look like he is winning. He may be jumping up and down for joy over a particular area of your life. However, God will always cause us to be triumphant if we stay in Christ Jesus. Remember, even when the enemy thinks he's winning, he's losing!

Becoming One
1. What does winning in Christ look like for your life?

2. How can you always stand for the truth?

No More Debates

Foolish questions and genealogies lead to strife.

I've been in situations where I perceived that the person just wanted an argument or they were trying to create a debate trap. When that happens, the individual often begins by twisting the original words to make them mean something different than what was intended, missing the point and spirit behind what was said, bringing about another meaning.

Why do we need to avoid debates?

This question could seem odd coming from someone who was a part of her high school Speech and Debate Team, and before you get any ideas of an overconfident, well-spoken student who couldn't wait to get on stage and give her speech, let me assure you, it was quite the opposite. I was drafted by an English teacher who had already spoken with the Speech and Debate Team Coach to have me join the students who were already selected.

Have you ever witnessed a person argue so convincingly for a particular point of view and then turn around and be able to give a compelling argument for the exact opposite point of view?

The thing about a debate is that the speaker is really saying that the hearers need to agree with them because they are right.

What if debaters took their ego or ability to convince people of what to agree with out of the picture?

What if they were just interested in reporting the truth and leaving people to make their own decisions?

Why is there such a strong need for everyone to agree with a debater's point of view?

Perhaps we are encouraged to avoid

debates because the truth has a way of speaking up for itself, and as the old saying goes, "the truth will eventually come out."

Becoming One

1. Why is there such a strong need for everyone to agree with a debater's point of view?

2. How can you avoid debates?

Betrayal

Judas proves that just because a person is around and has access to the word of God, it doesn't necessarily mean they are saved. No one really knows what is going on inside a person. A person could be going through the motions or have an ulterior motive.

One cannot serve God and mammon.

We see that Judas' allegiance was to mammon. He was a thief, and his closeness to Jesus was all about what He could get out of the deal. Ultimately, Judas wanted to know how he could steal from people.

No one discerned that Jesus would be betrayed–except Jesus Himself. Each person began to ask the Lord, am I going to betray you? (Matthew 26:17-30).

This means that Judas looked like the real deal. Otherwise, if it were apparent, the disciples would have asked, "Lord is it Judas who will betray you?"

You know your friends!

When someone describes someone by sharing something they said or did without providing a name, you immediately know who they are referring to based on the description.

The point is, when you feel lost or know something is not right in your heart, don't just try to "go along, to get along." The enemy will use your response to push you further and further until you find yourself selling out for 30 pieces of silver (like Judas).

Judas could have asked Jesus for the 30 pieces of silver. After all, Jesus paid Peter's taxes and showed him how to catch a boatload of fish. Jesus didn't have money problems. Everything needed was always provided. You'll find a large upper room furnished; go there and prepare our meal (Luke 22:12). You'll find a colt tied up; tell them I need it (Luke 19:30).

All Judas had to do was talk with

Jesus. Yes, it might be awkward to say, Jesus, I love money more than I love you. I want to use you to benefit myself. However, Jesus already knows the truth. We are not fooling Him one second. Jesus would likely have told Judas, all that I have is yours (Luke 15:31).

Never run away from Jesus because He is the solution. God has the answer to all our problems.

Becoming One
1. Is there an area of your life where you are pretending to have it together, although you are struggling?

2. Are you willing to ask for help? If you keep going the way you're going, where will it lead you?

Spiritual Wickedness in High Places

The enemy often appears as an angel of light to distract and move us out of alignment and being one with God. Therefore, we have to beware of how not to fall into the tricks, traps, and schemes of the enemy.

Fortunately, God can make us aware of these ploys to keep us on track through His gift of discernment. God may also warn us of wolves in sheep's clothing, of false prophets, and those with ulterior motives who will ultimately pull us away from intimacy and oneness with God.

For example, there is a special facility that serves as a library, theater and exhibit museum all rolled into one. My kids have been there many times to watch the theatrical performances and participate in the interactive fanfare—it's aways a pleasant experience.

Once, I had a dream about being inside the building. Everything was beautiful, well-lit and people smiling and enjoying themselves. In an instant like the flip of a switch, there was a dim and somber atmosphere.

There was a clergyman wearing his black suit with the white collar. He stood in the loft looking down as he leaned over the balcony.

I stood on the bottom floor and what seemed like hundreds of black, tiny, little shadowy spirits began to surround me. The clergyman observed the scenario as the black spirits got closer and closer, attempting to lure me into the theater, and put something inside me.

I awoke screaming to the top of my lungs, "Get out of my body! Get out of my body!"

Jumping out of bed, I began to pace

the floors and went into intense prayer, which some call spiritual warfare.

I believe what the Lord showed me through this dream was the concept of this angel of light. Everything can look innocent and fun, and just when we are comfortable and at ease, the script is flipped. Light becomes darkness.

There is a Godly veneer in the clergy garment and collar, but in my dream, it's this very image that is "overseeing" the wicked spirits, as he stood in the loft where the vain imaginations were exalted and fighting against the true knowledge of God.

Every one of the imps in my dream represented thoughts or ideologies wanting to hold a higher place than the Word of God.

These demon spirits are trying to get us into the theater to engage in pretense, performance, or spectating—all of which will draw us out of alignment with God.

This dream served as a warning for the believer and the church. There are things from the heart of Satan that don't belong in the Body of Christ. We can't be tricked by the outward righteous veneer.

The bible speaks of those who would appear to be Godly, but inwardly they are ravening wolves. As a body of believers, we must begin to cast out everything that does not align with the word of God out of our lives and out of the Body of Christ.

We must take authority over spiritual wickedness in high places, so we are free to be one with God.

We must love God with all our heart, soul, mind and strength and not just pretend to love Him while others are watching. We have to rely on the grace of God to empower us to be one with Him, and not rely on our own performance.

Finally, the bible speaks of joints supplying the joints. This phrase means we are all called to benefit from one another with the gifts God has given us.

Therefore, we can't sit in the theater seats and be passive in our pursuit of oneness. We must be actively involved in God's Kingdom.

Becoming One

1. Can you recognize when someone around you pretends to be a true friend but operates as an enemy?

2. Have you paid attention to the warnings God gives you concerning the subtle enemy?

Angel of Light

In one of my dreams, I saw a man in the family room. It seemed like he was part of the family—like a father figure. He seemed good-natured and friendly. He smiled and conversed intimately with the family.

As the dream continued, I remember walking the streets at night. The man stood over to the left. Police were randomly stopping people and checking their phones for codes. The man was calm and asked a couple of young ladies on the street if the police had started checking their phone codes. He was ecstatic that the codes were released and began smiling and jumping up and down for joy.

Then it became clear that this man was pretending to be nice and friendly but was excited about what he thought would be the people's demise.

In a moment of stillness, it became known that somehow the codes were changed by someone higher up, a Higher Power. When the man realized the codes were changed and his diabolical plan would not work, he became furious. Just as he had jumped up and down with joy, he started to stomp and jump up and down with fierce vigor and anger.

The Lord revealed to me that sometimes, the subtle enemy might look like he is winning in our lives. He may be jumping up and down for joy over a particular area of our life. However, God will always cause us to be triumphant if we stay in Christ Jesus.

Remember, even when it looks like the enemy is winning, he's not. He is actually losing! No one can curse what God has blessed.

The enemy's power is rented from you! He can make suggestions, but it's up to you to take the bait. If you don't take the bait, you remain in the winner's circle.

Everyone will have an opinion of you. It doesn't make it true. They can testify against you in a court of law, but it still doesn't make it true.

Remember Jesus, how they called Him a devil?

When they call you names and make false accusations against you, remember, after your crucifixion moments, you will rise in even greater power.

Silence is golden when you're going through tough times and dealing with challenging people. A fast from words and a dependence on God to advocate for you and raise you is needed in the evil day, the day of testing. Our Father will not allow the angel of light to deceive us. Keep your eyes on Jesus, the author and finisher of our faith.

Becoming One
1. What will you do to ensure your power is not relinquished to the angel of light?

2. How will you maintain your focus on God in times of testing or when the angel of light attempts to orchestrate your demise?

Prayer to Become One

Father God, we turn away from all things that are not of you, and we turn towards you. Our eyes are upon you,

you rescue us from all sins and every plan of the enemy. Lord God, thank you that we can safely run to you.

We command the enemy to flee from us seven different ways. We command his powers to be ineffective and inoperable in our lives in the name of Jesus. We see the enemy afar off, and we hide ourselves in you, so He has no effect on us. Father, we lift our shield of faith, and we quench every fiery dart that the enemy throws our way.

Lord, it's not by our might or strength,

but by your power and anointing. God you are releasing shackles right now, and delivering and letting the captives go free.

Thank you for our families, and we declare it is well with our homes. Lord, it is well in our cities, our churches, and our states. We dwell in safety and peace because we know who we belong to. We are your children. We've been bought with a price, and none can harm us or make us afraid. Our trust, hope, and our lives are in hid in you, Christ Jesus.

Thank you for every provision you made for us. Thank you for all power and authority that you have given us. You've made us to sit in heavenly places with Christ Jesus, and we tread over all serpents, scorpions, the power of the enemy, and spiritual wickedness in high places.

You call us to rule and reign by Christ Jesus. Thank you for bringing us into divine alignment, in the name of Jesus. The enemy is losing his grip and his power.

We are not afraid of the future,

persecution, or to be called the children of God, and we won't be afraid Father God to speak your gospel and your truth. We won't be afraid to stand on your word and to contend for the faith. We will not be ashamed of your gospel for it is the power of God unto salvation.

We won't be captured by this world's system. Thank you, God, that you still the hand of the enemy and the avenger. No weapon that is formed against us will prosper and every tongue that arises against us in judgment, you will condemn it. In Jesus' name, Amen.

One Message

One Message

The Holy Spirit speaks to us in dreams. In my mind, these dreams are modern-day parables. A parable is a story told with vivid images that teach profound truths and have deeper meanings when examined beyond the surface level. Parables are life stories that convey spiritual messages.

When God reveals visions and dreams, He often shares something about our past, future, or the people around us. Many times, God has messages for us individually and even corporately as a local body of believers, and sometimes it's for the church or world at large.

We can receive answers to prayers, directions, and even warnings from God through dreams.

<u>**Our Prayer**</u>

Our Father,
who art in heaven,
hallowed be thy name;
thy kingdom come;
thy will be done
on earth as it is in heaven.
Give us this day our daily bread;
and forgive us our trespasses
as we forgive those who trespass against us;
and lead us not into temptation,
but deliver us from evil.
For thine is the Kingdom
And the power and the glory
Forever. Amen.

Forerunner

There was a period when I felt very close to the Lord. I made the sacrifice to be at every prayer meeting, practically every time it was offered. I remained attentive to every word the person who prayed said.

I agreed and prayed that the Lord would give me the scriptures to pray that harmonized with the prayer leader. We had great sensitivity to the Spirit of God. When we showed up, we didn't rush to pray. We spent time at the altar and waited until the presence of the Lord came upon me.

During that time, we weren't just praying our words or memorizing scriptures. It was like a pump priming prayerful words out of us. When we felt the Spirit lift, we would remain quiet and listen.

Often, the Lord spoke an encouraging word to our hearts. Sometimes we had conversations about feeling like we were in a different space.

Those experiences led me to want to know God more personally, but in other circles, I began to feel like I was sticking out like a sore thumb.

I wanted to blend in, but I just didn't. I attempted to water down my prayers and worship and stopped carrying my Bible with me everywhere I went. At that time, I didn't want to be viewed as a "Holy roller."

I tried hard to tone it down. However, every time I think about the mercy of God to choose me for life and not for evil, to cover my sins with His blood, to make an escape for me when there was no other way, tears of gratitude pour out of me.

Understanding that I will never measure up to God's holiness on my own, and I have Jesus taking the bullet for my sins, moves me in an indescribable way.

I mentioned that I tried to put a little space between God and me so I could blend in better with those around me. After all, I needed to be relatable. I also didn't want to draw attention to myself.

I really am not comfortable in the spotlight. I didn't want to be viewed as spooky or religious, but I wouldn't have said this at the time, and it took a revelation to conclude, but I valued the opinion of people more than I valued the presence and anointing of God. After a prayer meeting, one of the intercessors said to me, "Nikki, you just can't blend."

Those words gripped me, and I became more comfortable with not fitting in over the years. Don't sacrifice your relationship with God for anything or anyone. The cost is too great, and the consequences are too dire. Choose to be one with the Father. He has gone before us to secure our ability to commune with God.

Becoming One
1. Where have you experienced insecurity in your relationship with God?

2. What have you now accepted, knowing Christ is your forerunner?

High School Track Dream

I had a dream and saw myself in my high school track team's uniform. I ran at a steady and swift pace. However, as I looked around, I noticed I was the only one running.

Perplexed, I started to doubt myself and where I was headed. What was all this running for anyway?

Did I get off track?

Where was everyone?

I saw a nice, shaded seating area off to the side. I stopped with heavy breathing and hands resting on my knees, contemplating my next move.

After some time had passed, a herd of

people ran toward me in their track uniforms. I could see their numbers pinned on them.

Suddenly, facing the wrong way, I seemed to have no energy to start running again. The entire group ran right past me, leaving me in the dust.

When God calls us to a specific task, we may be the only person at first.

Don't get discouraged, confused, or slack off because no one seems to be where you are. Maybe they just haven't seen what God has shown you.

Hebrews 12:1-2 reads, "Therefore, since we are surrounded by such a great cloud of witnesses, let us throw off everything that hinders and the sin that so easily entangles.

And let us run with perseverance the race marked for us, fixing our eyes on Jesus, the pioneer and perfecter of our faith. For the joy set before Him, he endured the cross, scorning its shame, and sat down at the right hand of the throne of God."

Run your race! Keep your eyes on Jesus.

Becoming One

1. What race are you running?

2. How will you stay motivated to continue moving forward?

Eagle Vision

One day in my kitchen, with my eyes wide open, I saw a picture of a lot of soldiers wearing gray uniforms marching forward. The sound as their steps hit the floor was precise, and they stood in perfect formation.

In front of them were officers with gray uniforms, and a yellow scarf was a part of their uniform and distinguished them as leaders.

Ahead of them, at a greater distance, I saw a General, who I recognized as my church pastor at the time. All the soldiers stood on a brilliant white floor. I noticed that the gray uniformed soldiers faced forward, but the officers with yellow uniforms faced each other.

The General made a gesture, and instantly, in one unified movement, all the soldiers moved and rose into the air, and they took the form of an eagle. The General, my pastor, became the head of the eagle, the leaders with the yellow scarves became the yellow feathers on the neck of the eagle, and the gray uniformed soldiers became the body of the eagle. It's as though the white became the sky, and the eagle flew off toward the sun.

When I had the vision, I shared it with my pastor. Initially, I thought it meant the leaders weren't confident and were looking at each other instead of looking and giving their full attention to the General. Shortly after the dream, our entire leadership team left the church at the same time.

As I spent time considering the dream and meditating on God's word, He revealed to me that He is assembling His army and His body of believers, and He wants us, as His leaders, to adjust ourselves so that they are looking forward toward Him—not to each other. We are to be in tight formation, awaiting the signal to soar as one unified body like an eagle.

When we look to man, there will be discouragement, and we will leave when things get tough. However, when we look to God, our Commander in Chief, He gives us staying power and ultimately causes us to soar in victory.

Becoming One
1. What is God showing you?

2. How has that vision impacted you?

Garments Matter

"The rules don't apply to me"—pride.

"God knows my heart"—stubborn.

We've likely heard these phrases at some point, and when we think this way, we are not wearing the proper garments.

The Bible talks about being clothed in humility (1 Peter 5:5), tender mercies (Colossians 3:12), and with a robe of righteousness (Isaiah 61:10). Therefore, when we think the rules don't apply to us, we dishonor the garments we are intended to wear.

Sometimes we feel entitled to hold grudges or unforgiveness in our hearts. However, God commands us to forgive others when they sin against us, and if we don't forgive, God will not forgive our sins (Matthew 6:14).

To wear the garments God commands can't be done in our strength. After all, our righteousness is like filthy rags (Isaiah 64:4). We need Jesus to exchange our dirty garments with His pure righteousness.

He is the only one without sin and qualified to cover us.

So be friendly and compassionate towards others, surrender your nature to God's will, and wear the garments that matter to Him. Our goal is to please the Father.

Becoming One
1. Which garment must you consciously wear?

2. How will you rely on the Holy Spirit to help you when your flesh wants to win?

Contend
for the Faith

I had a dream that I was in a big red church. The inside resembled a warehouse. Outside, there were two young Christians about to get into a fight.

Seeing the commotion, I went outside quickly. I told the older of them that they knew better and shouldn't be engaging in that behavior.

The individual swung through the air at the other Christian, and I couldn't tell if the person's chin was grazed or nearly missed.

I began to counsel the younger person, and the altercation ceased. There are reasons that we, as believers, swing at other believers. The one doing the swinging sometimes is also the one not listening to counsel.

Sometimes the one on the receiving end has to be the bigger person and receive the counsel to stop fighting amongst each other.

As believers, we should fight to contend for the faith, not against each other.

Often when we go through tests and trials, we can isolate ourselves, and then we start to think that what we face only happens to us because of who we are in God.

We start to think like Elisha when he was running away from Jezebel. Lord only, I am here to serve you. We must be careful not to shrink into our perspective.

God responds to Elisha that He has seven thousand men who have not bowed their knees to Baal. We have brothers and sisters all over fighting, praying, receiving persecution—contending for the faith of the Gospel.

We must see ourselves as a collective whole who must find a way to support each other as one.

Becoming One
1. How will you contend for the faith?

2. What has been one lesson you've learned along your faith journey?

You've Already Won

Satan, the accuser, would never have crucified the Lord if He knew adversity gave Him more power in the future. After Jesus' battle with His flesh, pain, and shame, He experienced all power and authority.

So, beloved Bride of Christ, don't get discouraged when you're attacked!

You've been told you are the problem, how ineffective you are, and how much power you lack. You have been conditioned to see yourself as a big mess that needs a lot of fixing and a great deal of help.

Remember, Adam and Eve had it all. They were in a beautiful garden; God came to personally meet with them every day. Couldn't they have waited and asked God for the knowledge they desperately wanted?

When God says don't touch something and don't eat something, it's for our good.

Don't try to work around Him–go to Him! Assess what is at stake when you fail to follow His instructions.

Beloved, you're already furnished for every good work. You're already dressed for success. You can't lose because the team has already won. The enemy's job is to get you in continual pursuit of what you already have.

The Greater One dwells within you. You're already seated in heavenly places and have authority over spiritual wickedness. Don't get weary; stay the course! You are a King's kid!

Becoming One

1. What lies from the enemy have you previously accepted as true? How will you turn those lies over to God?

2. What do you need to ask God for in this season? What area(s) of your life are you not discussing with Him?

Prayer to Become One

Father, you are the lifter of our heads, and the Kingdom of God is at hand. We are walking in power, a renewed vigor, and the fire of God will spread in the name of Jesus.

We make intercession for everyone who doesn't know or who does not experience the truth and power of your word. Thank you that they come into the knowledge of your truth.

We will be cities set upon a hill that cannot be hidden. Our lights won't go out, people will see your hand upon our lives as you make us lights and witnesses. We will have a word fitly spoken in our mouths that won't return void, as you send it out through us to accomplish salvation for households.

We are Kingdom citizens, citizens of another country. Therefore, we always do those things that please you. God, whatever we put our hands to do, we declare that it will prosper. We agree with the prayers of others that have already gone forth ahead of us. God, we believe that you will give us creativity, inventions, and witty ideas to win and bring in the lost. So that we may all be one in you and you in us. One will plant, and one will water, but you God, in the name Jesus will give the increase.

One Day

One Day

One day Jesus will return to take us to heaven with God our Father. Therefore, we must return to Him in order to expect His return. We must be ready (Matthew 24:44).

<u>Our Prayer</u>

Our Father,

who art in heaven,

hallowed be thy name;

thy kingdom come;

thy will be done

on earth as it is in heaven.

Give us this day our daily bread;

and forgive us our trespasses

as we forgive those who trespass against us;

and lead us not into temptation,

but deliver us from evil.

For thine is the Kingdom

And the power and the glory

Forever.

Amen.

No Longer Separated

Jesus said, "I have sheep that are not of this fold" (John 10:16).

Wait just a minute, did that statement send a jolt of surprise to Jesus' nearest followers?

Could they have thought that because they were with Jesus (practically every day) and had a firsthand account of what they saw Him doing, they were the only chosen ones?

Similarly, remember Peter sitting on the rooftop telling the Lord God of all creation that He wasn't going to touch anything unclean?

It's possible that the Jews thought they had something special going on with God and the Messiah, and they did. However, the problem was when God was ready to include outsiders, many of the Jews had no dealing with people who were not Jewish.

There was a time when a veil separated us as people from getting to an intimate place with God. We had to rely on a priest to go to God and make atonement for us.

Today, we go directly to God and pray.

Becoming One
1. What matters are you positioning before God?

2. Have you ever felt separated from God? What were the conditions?

The Two Shall Become One

As I walked into the living room of the little white house on Woodrow Ave., there was an unusual stillness in the air, and it appeared that no one else was home when I arrived, yet the tiny radio broadcast from the corner of the room where it sat, often ignored.

This afternoon, a male voice had the attention of the room. He announced a series of statistics on sex and marriage. He gave the percentages of people who were most satisfied with the sex in their marriage. The highest correlation of satisfaction remained with the couples who had not entered sexual relations before marriage.

The correlation of satisfaction continued to decrease for those couples who had sex before marriage, and the more partners they had before marriage, the less sexual fulfillment they reported in their marriage.

To be clear, I was shocked that people were talking about sex on the radio, but my teen ears were perched and soaking in every word.

The timing of the information for me couldn't have been better because my boyfriend had started pressuring me for sex.

Subconsciously, I knew sex would be the next step to prove my love, but I also knew teens weren't supposed to have sex before marriage. Yet, many of the kids my age were actively involved.

After hearing this broadcast, my mind was convinced. I was not going to sacrifice the sexual satisfaction of my future marriage for anyone. It was a logical decision for me.

"Lord, how am I going to tell my boyfriend that I am not having sex until I'm married?" I prayed.

To my surprise, he called and broke up with me over the phone. I was so relieved. I didn't give one word of protest. Looking back, I realized his ending the relationship was a tactic to get me to cry and beg him not to break up with me so that I would do anything to get him back, including having sex as I had known of so many other girls doing.

After a week, the football, basketball, and track star called me, saying He had made a mistake and wanted to restart our relationship. I quickly let him know he had made the right decision. I had already made up my mind that the next person I dated would be a person who was a viable candidate for marriage.

I was committed to making the necessary decisions to follow Christ all the way–becoming one with Him.

Becoming One
1. What tough decisions are you grappling with to prepare yourself to become one with God?

2. How do you withstand temptation and remain one with God?

The Day of Jezreel

I woke up one morning hearing the word "JEZREEL."

I had no idea what it meant, and I couldn't connect it to anything. However, I knew God was speaking to me, so I searched for the word throughout scripture.

I found out some amazing things:
1. There is a Day of Jezreel.
2. There is a place called Jezreel.
3. There is someone named Jezreel.

However, the Holy Spirit led me to the book of Hosea. Hosea 1:11 reads, "Then the children of Judah and the children of Israel shall be gathered together and appoint for themselves one head; and they shall come up out of the land, for great will be the day of Jezreel!"

It will be a great day when God's children gather together as one under the leadership, Lordship and love of God the Father, Jesus Christ the Son and the Holy Spirit.

Jezreel means God sows or may God give seed. Jesus is the seed that God sowed into the world. He gave His only begotten Son, that whoever would believe in Him would not perish but have everlasting life. God's sends His message of love to us over and over again in so many different ways until we get it.

God cries out. I love you; I sent my son Jesus to die for you. Even when you didn't accept me and sinned and were called not my people, I made the choice to love you and changed not my people, to My people.

I made a new covenant with you so you wouldn't have to go through a priest or preacher. I decided to put my words and laws in your heart. You have heard me calling out to you. I have my hands stretched out to you. I am calling you Jezreel, you are my people. Will you come to me? Will you let me love you? will you let me save you? Will you open the door of your heart to me and fellowship with me when I knock on the door of your heart? Will you let Me, the King of Glory come in and dine with you? I have so many things to teach you and share with you. How to make your life work. How to help and inspire others. How to measure what really counts in life. You are my chosen. I choose you, Jezreel, will you choose me? Will you unite and become one with me?

Becoming One

1. How does making God the head of your life show up in your daily actions?

2. How is your confidence impacted by knowing God will return for you?

Prayer to Become One

Holy and Gracious Father, we bless and praise you! We come into agreement that the Body of Christ at large and individually will make itself ready for the return of our Lord and Savior, Jesus Christ by faith and diligent action.

We confess and repent of all our sins.

We yield to the process of washing our garments and removing the spots and wrinkles.

We submit ourselves to your agape love, not our will, but your will be done in us and through us. Let the lost come in by the droves, let the taste of sin be no longer pleasing. We will begin to say let us think logically about this, although my sins are like crimson, I know that Jesus can make them white as snow. The blinders are removed, Lord, and we are uncomfortable in and with sin.

Thank you for redeeming the lost, for saving souls, and for forgiving sins. Thank you for having mercy upon us Father. Give us the grace to obey you and love you and others. Let us be ready for the day when we meet you face to face in, Jesus' name. Amen.

Acknowledgements

JT Publishing House, thank you– especially Jossalyn Wilson. Jossalyn's professionalism and dedication to bring this book to print was above and beyond.

Jovania George, my in house critic, thank you so very much for sharing the truth in love.

Author's Bio

Nikki George is the author of Secret Place Poems and a children's book, Speak It: God's Confessions for Me.

She has actively served in children's ministry for years and loves to help the younger generation develop their identity in Christ. George streams and hosts The "i" Witness Show with Nikki George. She is also the owner of NikkiNovelties and Write Company Publishing.

The University of North Carolina at Charlotte Alumna is also an ordained Minister and has been blessed to have 28 years of marriage. She and her husband Maurice are the parents of seven children and have two grandchildren.

Nikki's mission is to help turn the hearts of the children back to the Father and be a witness that spreads the gospel of Jesus Christ throughout the world.